The Fire Landscape

The Fire Landscape

Poems by
Gary Fincke

The University of Arkansas Press
Fayetteville
2008

ISBN-10: 1-55728-881-X
ISBN-13: 978-1-55728-881-3

12   11   10   09   08   1   2   3   4   5

Designed by Liz Lester

⊛ The paper used in this publication meets the minimum requirements
of the American National Standard for Permanence of Paper for Printed
Library Materials Z39.48—84.

LIBRARY OF CONGRESS CATALOGING-IN-PUBLICATION DATA

Fincke, Gary.
    The fire landscape : poems / by Gary Fincke.
        p.   cm.
    ISBN 978-1-55728-881-3 (pbk. : alk. paper)
    I. Title.
    PS3556.I457F57   2008
    811'.54—dc22
                            2008018608

As always,

for Liz

ACKNOWLEDGEMENTS

Grateful acknowledgement is made to the editors of the following publications in which these poems originally appeared: "The Anomaly Museum," "The Pause in the Plummet for Prayer," and "The 1918 House," *The Gettysburg Review*; "The Good War," "The Privacy of the Hands," and "Filling in the Maps" (part 3), *The Saint Ann's Review*; "Black Veils," "The Horns of Guy Lombardo," "Like Ours," "White Gloves," "The Casual Slurs," "This," "Snickering like the Pharisees," and "Something like the Attic," *Prairie Schooner*; "The Sorrows" and "Late August," *Poetry Northwest*; "Queen for a Day" (broadside) and "The Shooting" (as sections in *The Lengthening Radius of Hate), Cervena Barva Press*; "The Fire Landscape," *Firefly*; "House Call," "Girdles," and "Because It Was Always Summer," *Paterson Literary Review*; "The Fluoroscope Era," *Columbia Poetry Review*; "Them!. . . and second big feature . . . Tarantula!" *The North American Review*; "Dunce," "The Impossible," "May, 1970," and "The Empowerment of Trust," *The Literary Review*; "The Coonskin Cap" and "Skill," *Poet Lore*; "The Salk Years" (as sequence) and "Such Places," *The Southern Review*; "Bomb Drill," *West Branch*; "Porch Moths" and "The Theory of Dog Shit," *Weber Studies*; "Watching the Tied Girl," *Southern Poetry Review*; "False Dawn," *Michigan Quarterly Review*; "Filling in the Maps" (part 3), *The Modern Language Review*; "Decorative Food" and "Elegy: The Properties of Blood," *Smartish Pace*; "English Class Report: I Married a Monster from Outer Space," *The Journal*; "Glitter Stars," *Cincinnati Poetry Review*; "The Shooting" (as sequence), *Zone 3*; "The Barter System," *Pleiades*; "History Bites," *Beloit Poetry Journal*; "Love Poem for the Dying," *Kestrel*; "The Ghosts in the Shelter," *River Styx*; "This," *Poetry Daily*; "Heavy Fog, December," *The Laurel Review*; "Miracles," *Fine Madness*, and "History Bites" (in *Blood Ties), Time Being Books*.

CONTENTS

The Fire Landscape

The Anomaly Museum

The Anomaly Museum

My mother believed in the prophecy
Of metaphors, how the anomalous
Foretold the promises of the body,
And she cited the child, with fur, just born,
The woman who had grown a forehead horn,
And, most telling, the boy whose head ballooned
To show us salvation's fortunate sign.

"To make room," she said. "To accommodate
His beautiful, enormous soul," meaning
For me to consider my thoughts, turning
My headaches into hope and fear, making
Wonder from misery so rare, the way
A reader might take these syllabic lines
As one more expression of *Look at me,*
Each word a disguise for deformity,
Like the airbrushed nudes in the night museum
Of magazines I toured during high school.

Then, while my mother's heart turned commonplace
With disease, I entered classrooms to face
The exhibits for terrible fortune:
The boy with Thalidomide stumps, the boy
Bent breathless by tumor, the girl whose lungs
Thickened to failure—Kevin and Rob, Greer.
I can recollect their names thirty years
After I passed by their symbolic selves
In the hall of occasional horror.

All along, my cousins were carrying
Their latent, faulty genes toward the three sons
Who would show that flaw in their sluggish brains,
Those boys calling up the face of that child
Who disappeared inside the great swelling
Of rare luck, the impossible size meant
To console us who need only foresee
The common routes to death, the stroke, this week,
That froze one side of a friend, his voice gone
To the slurred vowels of my cousins' boys.

The truth is that yesterday my friend still
Inhabited such a possible face
I looked everywhere he wasn't. And now,
In the museum I visit by myself,
I examine the bleak pornography
Of anomaly, attentive to how
The plates of one childish skull expanded
Until they burst open like a flower,
So impossible there is not one thing
To do but think of the boy as blossom,
Disregarding the ordinary parts
Of him until I imagine his heart's
Delicate, doomed pulse exposed, surfacing
On the swollen sea of brain like the drowned.

The Fluoroscope Era

How the Good War Ended

The first day held the immense dawn
Of a second sun. My mother
Kept wailing to herself and pushed
While my father believed, sitting
In another room, that nothing
Was more important than a son.

Now, memory was important.
He lifted a Pittsburgh paper
From a waste basket and printed
The name he'd picked by the weather.
"There," he said, "the very first thing,"
And folded it like a newsboy
To tuck the perfect word inside.

He was planning to improve me
Like a product. After four years
I was old enough to follow
The newsreel of how the good war
Had ended. The next one, I heard,
Would be made of eternity.

I sat small between my parents,
My fingers turning beautiful
From the salted nuts my mother,
Who was beginning to die, passed
To me like all of her cravings.

Black Veils

I learned the verse where God demanded hats,
Found the reference to veils. For hundreds
Of Sundays, the women around me were
Covered by the lacy, black strands of tulle.

I saw that men can show their face to God,
Learned that faith surrounds the heart like cotton.
Without it I would hear my pulse, go mad.
The dead were delivered at once or damned.

The veils were raised by hymns; they fell for prayer,
Fluttered through the long words of the pastor
As if something frail and invisible
Were beating its wings against the fine threads.

The dark veils were as serious as smoke.
They whispered the soft language of the dead—
Mrs. Shelby, Miss Swope—I knew the names
Like the books of the Bible, Genesis

To Revelation. When I tried one on,
I sensed the dim humility of hope.
When I examined myself in mirrors,
The clothes I wore needed to be undone.

The Sorrows

Whatever the Sunday, the sorrows kept the women
    in the kitchen,
My cousins and their mothers, my grandmother, her sister,
    all of them
Foraging through the nerves for pain. They sighed and rustled
    and one would
Name her sorrows to cue sympathy's murmurs, the first
    offerings
Of possible cures: three eggs for chills and fever,
    the benefits
Of mint and pepper, boneset, sage, and crocus tea.
    Nothing they
Needed came over-the-counter or through prescriptions
    not bearing
A promise from God, who blessed the home remedies
    handed down
From the lost villages of Germany for the aunt
    with dizzy spells,
For the uncle with the steady pain of private swelling;
    for passed blood,
For discharge and the sweet streak from the shoulder.
    In the pantry,
Among pickled beets and stewed tomatoes, were dark,
    honeyed liquids,
The vinegar and molasses sipped from tablespoons
    for sorrows
So regular they spoke of them as laundry to be smoothed
    by the great iron

Of faith which sets creases worthy of paradise. And there,
when only
A hum came clear, they might have been speaking from clouds
like the dead,
But what mattered when the room went dark were the voices
reaching into
The lamp-lit living room of men who listened then, watching
the doorway
And nodding at the nostrums offered by the tongues
of the unseen
As if the sorrows were soothed by the lost dialect
of the soul,
Which whispered to the enormous ache of the imminent.

Queen for a Day

After we clapped loudest for the woman
Whose two sons had been killed in Korea,
After she cried and accepted her crown,
Our mother gave us her weekday warning
For our two hours alone, saying her prayer
Against matches, glass, and a three-story
Fall through windows. Our father was asleep
In the attic—*Don't wake him. If someone
Knocks on the door, be still until he leaves.*
Our troubles: nothing that would win a crown
Unless our father tiptoed out the door
Or the wiring shorted sparks up the wall.

Our two hours alone were like listening
To the slow readers, how, during their turns,
Even the two syllables for colors
Sawed to stumps like the arm of Jimmy Koch—
Yehhhhhh and puhhhhhh, those simple sounds extending
Like lost fingers reaching through vowel-filled air.
Hardship was only the end of choices.
Our mother taught us *Private* for all things
That made us sad. We locked ourselves inside,
Listened up the stairs for breathing, and turned
Off the television, imagining
A beautiful hopelessness to clap for.

Drawing the Soul

"Imagine your soul," Miss Shuker said,
"How beautiful its shape when it leaves
Your body to seek your angel self."
She led us to the stained glass window
For Ascension, Christ among the doves,
The sky surrounding him like a veil.
"Draw light," she said. "Draw joy without wings
For you shall have them," and Linda Roy
Drew a yellow circle while Dave Trask
Fashioned a feathered orange arrow
On the heavy construction paper
We cut with our Sunday School scissors,
Each pair painted red with rounded tips
And the warning not ever to point
Because they were dangerous as guns.

A soul, I knew, weighed almost nothing,
Or else I'd feel it inside my heart,
And I drew dust, one piece light enough
To rise, Miss Shuker saying "snowflake"
And smiling as we pasted our souls
Below the cloud where she'd drawn a hand
That reached down for our flowers and stars,
The loose sleeve at its wrist so golden
We imagined Jesus on his knees
To take us through the floor to heaven
Just above the thick paper's edge where
We couldn't see, even when she held
Our soaring souls up to the window,
Bathing our futures in pastel light.

The Fire Landscape

Across the street, across the tracks and creek,
Across the cindered lot to where slag piles
Rose higher than the three second-floor rooms
We rented, Spang-Chalfant dumped heaps of flame.
From our unheated attic, my mother
Holding her breath and me, I leaned, some nights,
Through the small, stick-propped window's space to see.
Downstairs, space heaters glowed the red patterns
Of fire waffles. Two radiators hissed
And drooled and waited for the touch that made
Me suck away the sudden pain of sin.
In the cellar was a coal-fired furnace.
Below it was the open hearth of hell.

There, it was the flammable that mattered,
Myths of myself that tested the closed door
For a secret blaze, sniffed like a dog dazed
By strangers. Room after room was careless
With clutter. The radio hid embers;
The outlets housed their secret, open flames.
I listened to the saints of nails and glass,
The saints of bitterness, the saints of blood.
I became the saint of appliances,
Dreaming about twisted cords, waking
For the imminent flare of short circuits.

So many plugs to pull, switches to check.
The shift, by inches, of things from sources
Of heat. My mother and I searched each room

Before leaving, never once forgetting,
Not even a low-watt bathroom light bulb.
Some nights my father would drive us north where
Farms were turning into streets of houses,
Each lot a chance I'd live among children
Who thought steel was dug from the ground like coal.
When we moved, my room was so black I dreamed
Myself dead, woke and went to my window
Where the darkness convinced me I was right,
And I stopped breathing, waiting to see where
I was traveling, toward which kind of light.

House Call

A stranger opened his bag by my feet.
In the doorway, my mother rustled
like a curtain. The doctor looked
younger than my father, who was
playing dart ball in a church basement
because it was Monday and nothing
he could do would make a difference.

I was learning I wouldn't grow out
of this, that the house was full of threats:
dust, down pillows, books beside my bed.
My father, the baker, breathed flour
and never coughed, but I was joining
the sissies who were treated for flaws.

The doctor who never called again
sat on the bed and heard the secrets
in my chest. When he said "heart murmur,"
my mother closed the door so the house
couldn't hear. "Bronchial tubes," he said.
"Lungs. Throat." He mentioned mouth breathing
as if it would fill my body
with unknowable, lethal parts.
I was learning a man could calmly
explain himself. I was learning
the melody of a steady voice.
My mother listened and listened.
Her ears were so near to this song
she held her breath through every note.

The Fluoroscope Era

While I counted the limpers and hobblers,
The crutches, the canes, and the chairs on wheels,
My mother said the future was inside
My shoes, that I could be fitted by light.

My mother, who believed white shirts and ties
Were earned, trusted my walk to the wisdom
Of the carefully dressed, the dark-suited
Like Mr. Eck, who brushed the fluoroscope

While he studied the bright bones of my feet.
"What you have isn't cancer," he murmured;
"It's not the beginning of World War III,"
And I blinked like a doll, remembering

How boys, when the bomb fell in my comics,
Were skeletons and then nothing at all,
The sky over the earth turning as green
As the heavens on another planet

Or my feet inside new, corrective shoes.
The fluoroscope was the future, its time
Marked on Mr. Eck's radium watch, wound
And running accurately in the dark,

Flooding my feet in the green broth of size
To come if the Russians didn't destroy
The brilliance of my body. I squinted
And stared to the bone, reminding myself

That anybody could be alien,
Slew-footed by the chance of birth, dancing
The secret ballet of the built-up arch
Until the well-dressed declared you perfect.

Them!. . . and second big feature . . . Tarantula!

"Close your ears," Aunt Margaret said.
Across from the Homestead Theater
The sidewalk swarmed with strikers
Buzzing *hell* and *damn.* "Like this," she said,
Slapping her hands to her ears,
But I heard *bitch* and *bastard* before
She bought our way inside where huge ants
Were working their claws as they burned.

"The End" said we'd entered an hour late.
In minutes, an enormous spider
Stalked the screaming, slaughtering
Some of the slow-footed until it
Was fire-bombed, this time from jets.

When the ants returned, my aunt muttered,
"We know what happens to them,"
And tugged me to the door by the screen.
Over my head, a woman
Ten times my size stood hypnotized by
A set of enormous eyes.
Outside, at twilight, the strike-closed mill
Had turned radioactive,
Emptied by the bomb. Lifting their signs,
The men spread into traffic.

"Them!" my aunt said, as if steelworkers
Were giants, as if they would
Destroy Pittsburgh and devour us all.

Dunce

Because imperfection banished me to
The corner where the ordinary sat,
Dunce was the name I could be called each time
I wore that fool's cap all morning, my legs
Dangling from the high stool like a toddlers'.
Nothing was different about the voices
Of recitation, the shuffling of shoes.
Just to my left, numbers were divided
With chalk, quotients recorded and approved,
While I faced forward, a scuffed-out answer.

Dunce lasted. *Dunce* didn't disappear like
Difficult or *high strung, rebellious, loud.*
Dunce followed me to the playground, rode home
With me on the bus, an overnight guest.
The family said *dunce* so it sounded like
Blasphemy, like I was a minor god
Invoked in anger. "Dunce," they hissed, saving
Themselves from repeating the name of Christ.
I couldn't damn them to hell. All I did
Was become sacrifice in a sharp hat,
The temporary angel that saved them.

The Coonskin Cap

In the class photograph, the one
Where Miss Hartung stands to the side
So nobody in third grade is
Hidden behind her wide, black dress,
Jimmy Karras wears the fringe-trimmed
Jacket I thought about stealing
And Davy Crockett's coonskin cap.

My mother Scotch-taped that picture
To our white refrigerator.
"The poor boy," she said, though I thought,
Even then, she wanted to preach
About envy, fads, and water's
Danger to those who play alone,
Because Jimmy Karras drowned
In that coat the following day.

Instead, she walked me two miles north
To where Jimmy Karras had sunk.
There were tread-less tires, a box spring,
A refrigerator a child could die in.

"Can you see him?" my mother said,
"Can you?" making me set my stance
Wider along the steep pitch
Of the bank above the creek that ran
Into the Allegheny on its way
To Pittsburgh and the Ohio,

The Mississippi, and the Gulf
Of Mexico, each an answer
On a map test, what Miss Hartung
Made us take, grading where we lived
And where we imagined living.

The Horns of Guy Lombardo

Because I am ten-years-old and unashamed,
Because I've played the trombone for a year
And can read songs from a book of standards,
I walk off our porch to play "Auld Lang Syne"
At midnight to my family's applause.

My parents must know that a year from now
I will refuse to play for our neighbors,
But this is how we spend the first two minutes
Of 1956, the year before
I would fret about sex and God's absence.

I am as confident as the flood light
That illuminates the black, simple notes
And casts shadows so dark on the driveway
I can see the slide extend and retract
Like the sluggish tongue of an ancient frog.

My father is about to be thirty-eight,
His nails, even on off-days, black with work.
That evening, he knows his bakery
Will fail, groceries filling with cheap bread
And cake mixes easy enough for fools.

My mother's body is beginning to sag
With the weight of her collapsing thyroid
And the heavy numbers of blood pressure,
But she smiles and begins to sing the words
Like someone who expects to recover.

The snow, I imagine, is softening
My tone, making me sound as mellow as
The horns of Guy Lombardo, what the rest
Of the world kisses along to unless
They have stumbled outside at midnight, close

Enough to catch my song, hearing something
Like resolutions flung into the air.

The Salk Years

While Salk Tested

We walked past the basement storage room waist-high with coal that only the janitor who limped could touch. Outside, every heated day, soot settled on swings and slides that smeared our grade-school play. When we learned the janitor locked his door to smoke, our teacher said the worries of men earned them comfort, that we would learn that truth when we needed to. The summer before, my father had revised my life by building a house on Cherrywood Drive. Through July and August, he insisted I scald my hands before each meal to keep diseases of dirt away. "Typhoid," he said. "Polio." Tired in the legs was a life sentence; running each night was a test for weakness.

The contagious luck of iron-lung children spread through the mail. The father of a polio child talked during church, saying his daughter had played in her sandbox the day before she'd gotten sick. "I'd built that thing," he murmured, "and that night I tore it apart, burning every board before I wheeled the white sand to the woods." That man, my father explained, was crazy to believe polio came from sand. When I shuffled into fifth grade, he said, "Pick your feet up or they'll think you're crippled." Richard Hartman, the next week, changed into a victim. His desk disappeared. Two boys slid forward. Days later, the janitor limped it to the back of the row, sanded, revarnished, good as new.

Moonbows

"Not just yet," my father said, meaning
He wanted to see if Salk had it right,
His vaccine, and I wouldn't cramp to
A cripple from taking the unforeseen.
"Not just yet," though Salk's tests had started
In Pittsburgh, no side effects for a year
While my father encouraged baseball
And recognizing God's hand in the sky
Where night rainbows, so shy, needed mist
Thick from waterfalls and a moon risen
Nearly full behind us to form white arcs.
And he told me how, at Pennsylvania's
Highest falls, people arrived so early
They had hours to choose the section of sky
Where they imagined that angel would form
Like some sign promised to them by scripture,
How his father watched until the moon
Reached the angle for pale beauty to show
Itself in the spray. My father, a boy,
Being held by his father, who lowered
His voice as if sound needed to be dimmed
Like light to earn such radiance, even
As stars were erased by the abrasion
Of cities, the sky smothered by smog, hearts
Darkened by the interference of news.

Bomb Drill

That first year our grade school hugged basement walls
To save ourselves from the H-bomb, I thought
My teacher looked old enough to die
If nothing fell from the Pittsburgh sky.

She had grayer hair than my grandmother
Who was already dead; she could have been
On my Sunday school program cradling
Children in her arms and repeating

Old women's prayers against brimstone, smiling
As we climb the splintered and slanted stairs
To refill our classrooms like water.
Now, each plane made me foresee the first

Tumbling bomb while my classmates were singing
"America" as if it were something
Besides curriculum. Stevenson,
Campaigning, said *restraint* and *reason*

On television while I was sitting
In Bob Shereba's game room, and I heard
His old man say, "Fuck you," to the screen.
I looked to see what was more obscene

Than the bomb, but there were just words. He took
Us downstairs. He showed us bottled water,

The cans of Spam, and the radio
That marked all the frequencies for woe.

"You listen to this," he said, and I heard
Construction, jackhammers. There were spiders
On the walls; there was a shell so dry
In a giant, corner web I tried

To figure what flavor it might have been.
I stared at the cinderblock he'd painted
Powder blue because it said *comfort*,
What they'd need, more than likely, for years,

That shelter constructed for a half-life
My teacher said we couldn't understand,
Her hair, under the fluorescent light,
Turning an uncomfortable blue.

Bad Time

The president was having a bad time of it,
and so was I. In church. In school. Delivering
newspapers that said *ileitis* door to door.

"A heart attack, now this," my father said, citing
the surgery Ike required the week I finished
fifth grade with "needs to improve" in citizenship.

When I batted, coiled, and cocked like Stan Musial,
my father told me I looked like Nixon waiting
for a fat pitch he could hammer to the White House.

And my mother? After each game, she checked for ticks
because didn't I know we were things that fed them,
publicizing our blood with sweat and heat and breath?

"Look," my father said, "He'll get over it," meaning
it wasn't polio, that I was saved like Ike,
who ran again, giving Nixon four years to wait.

By November I'd learned one tick in a million
finds food enough to survive, that the ambush tick
has to sit on plants until something sweeps close by.

Such anticipation. Such need for the fortune
of blood. And if, miraculously, a warm thing
passes, there are a thousand ticks whose legs are poised.

That smell, so close, means some of them will live, and now
one tick leaps, followed by another, taking to
the air with the insistent vote of altitude.

Snickering like the Pharisees

After he led two hymns, after he said,
"Good morning in God's name," Waldo Braughler
Read a Bible passage, a parable
Or a history that celebrated
The same Sunday each year like a birthday.
I had perfect attendance, so I knew
Zacheus in the tree was October,
The second Sunday, that the last worker
Hired for the vineyard would earn equal pay
In the middle of May, understanding
Those stories were lessons about the ways
We needed God, while I watched the spaces
Between the buttons on the tight white blouse
Of Dolores Daugherty, the gleaming
White thigh of Connie Metz, dropping one dime
Into the offering and keeping one
For myself, repeating my own story
Of lust and greed, certain I could repent
Like the thief on the cross, be forgiven
Like the Prodigal Son if I could make
Myself say *I'm sorry,* open my mouth
As I did for hymns, lip-synching the words
To the earnest voice of Waldo Braughler,
My lips forming penance, then snickering
Like the Pharisees when Waldo started
Paul on the road to Damascus because
I had learned it was epilepsy, not
The bright light of God that converted him.

Porch Moths

As the world became pointless, I did nothing
differently, dressing for church and school,
bowing my head, raising my hand to answer.

Without symbols, sermons were postcards that kept
arriving like mail while my father
kept teaching our yard, our porch, the closest woods,

assigning me the nearby, natural world
to memorize, names I recited
the way I mumbled the words of hymns and creeds.

I didn't descend anywhere but the porch
where one bulb glared because the fixture
had cracked. In July, I still sat in the dark

or under a cluster of moths that believed,
he said, a lamp is the moon, choosing
their course from its light, keeping it angled to

their right, and then, too close to be guided, trapped
in circles, that warm moon holding them
with the false hope of instinctive paths.

Watching the Tied Girl

American, I thought it was, to help
Bob Shereba tie his sister against
A tree in the state preserve. "Commie spy,"
He said, and she needed to be left there
Because she would never confess or cry.
I didn't ask *Who's untying the Red?*
While we hiked home. I was busy keeping
Branches from my eyes. There were jagged leaves
That opened my legs, thorned brush we reached as
Anne Shereba screamed like no Soviet
I'd ever heard, tangling us where the path
Confused itself for a knotted moment.
Whatever Bob felt, I slipped back to watch.
I crouched until numbness edged up my legs;
I stood and expected the leaves to drop
Like a dancer's fan. During those minutes
Of staring, I heard myself swallow, thought
The flesh would rot from both of us before
The resolution of thoughtless bondage.

That night, alone at eleven, I watched
The story of a scientist turned mute
By secret pain. For twenty-five minutes,
Nothing helped because the doctors believed
He'd been driven to his madness by noise.
The heartless on this show were Communists,
But the scientist, a free-world hero,
Hadn't cracked and neither had the doctor
Who solved the case, deciding full silence

Made men lunatics for sound. He mentioned
Crickets, raindrops, the distant swish of cars.
He said the quietest place you know has
A comfort of sounds. And after they'd shocked
The patient back to sense, overloaded
Him with decibels, I sat in my room,
My parents an hour away, and heard all
The banalities of midnight, the creaks
And groans of stealth. I went to the window
Like the soon-to-be-murdered, looking for
The blade of the crazed, and saw that rescue
Relied on a vacuum, even the mites
Of sound sucked up, driven to some landfill
For bedlam where warnings were hooked and barbed.

The Privacy of the Hands

The summer before sixth grade, I believed
A hillside of trees meant we'd moved where wealth
And leisure lived, that college would call now
Like it had for the boy across the street
Who said the two of us should walk naked
In the darkness of trees behind his house.

Wasn't it exciting, he asked, to be
So free? Didn't I feel different nude?
"See?" he whispered. "See how I'm changed?" By then,
He was hard, but even when he touched me
I was soft and small, suddenly knowing
How skinny I was, how weak, that he could
Strangle me if that's what excited him.

Until that evening I'd thought the pleasure
Of touching myself was some privacy
I was alone in before I became
Someone who would stiffen and swell and seek
The darkness of women who would shudder,
But after his hand slipped away from me,
He stroked himself, crooning "Look now. Look now."

And I did, using the faint, back porch light
Of his house to see him explode between
My black tennis shoes, all I was wearing,
Not moving, but turning my head as if
I'd just murmured goodbye, as if he was
Standing in the open door of a train.

The Music of Ants

Even when he was naming the near woods
For me—*hickory, hemlock, beech,* and *ash*—
My father forgot my voice when I stood
To his right, murmuring *sure* and *ok,*
Un-huh, whatever while he repeated
Elderberry, sassafras, blue spruce, birch.
And I could recite a dictionary
Of obscenities now, from either side,
All sound smothered to confusion, but through
Those late Sunday afternoons, my father
Expected me to sense the grace of God
In twigs and leaves arranged into a test,
Teaching me the forest like times tables,
Automatic with shape and size, spouting
His rote products of insects, things to which
He listened like certain ants he lifted
To his left ear, the ones who wailed warnings
We can hear if we hold them close enough,
Kneeling on the earth to appreciate
Their miraculous ministry of sound,
Prophecies like the cricket songs that tell
The temperature through an old formula
As difficult to recall as the one
Converting Celsius to Fahrenheit.
Fractions, degrees, chirps per minute, screaming—
Broken down, the noises of nature scan

Like a sonnet. We can't help but listen
And count, listen and count, following sound
Until we anticipate the story,
Marveling at music we recognize
From hearing it repeated through our hearts.

False Dawn

My father shook me from sleep to say "Look,"
Directing me east toward a cone of light.
I thought he meant me to know the H-bomb
Had finally fallen, that our campground
Was fortunate to be a hundred miles
From Pittsburgh, even farther from New York,
The city I guessed was first to explode.
I stared at the end of the world, waiting
For him to explain what would follow, and
Because there was no moon, that glow faded
To the first question I managed, thinking
Radiation, "How far away was that?"
"How far away is the sun?" he answered,
Sounding so symbolic I expected
To be dead that day until he added,
"Now you can say you've seen something special."
At five a.m. I lay awake, telling
Myself there was a baseball game of time
Until sunrise, one inning already
Ended, the second started by strikeout.
"It's space debris," he murmured in the dark,
And I imagined the small particles
Of Earth drifting toward somebody who knew,
Like my father, what false dawn was, how dust
Could glow when aligned in the moonless night.
School would soon begin in Pittsburgh, still there,

And Miss Bell would elaborate, for sure,
On the canals of Mars, what she had taught
My sister the year before, how Martians
Had been so smart their incredible work
Could be seen from millions of miles away,
Yet they had vanished like the dinosaurs.

Filling in the Maps

Filling in the Maps

1

In sixth grade, in 1957,
History began with our presidents
In perfect order, their wars and with whom,
The dates for each from beginning to end.
We learned Democrats and Republicans,
Federalists, Whigs. In geography,
We named, in alphabetical order,
Each steadfast state before we recited
Their capitals: Albany, Atlanta,
Then Annapolis and Augusta, Maine.

So we could tell excellence from failure,
Miss Bell arranged our seats by weekly scores.
So we knew who loved our country, we learned
To label the conduits of rivers:
Arkansas and Gila, Potomac, Snake.
After those came mountains, following them
Our national parks, spelling important
Unless we wanted to suffer the scorn
Of the good citizens, those who had learned
All the names before us, not Communists
Who sought a score so much like average,
Not slackers, worse yet, who flunked to welfare.

2

The last hour of each day was art. While we painted, Miss Bell would sing all of the slow songs on *Your Hit Parade*. "Remember what weather looks like," she said. "Put something in your skies besides sun." Math was the five-minute subject. Numbers were homework. When we raised our hands, she said, "Ask your fathers," the fractions and decimals smeared to moments erased from the blackboard, becoming the shapes of clouds we added above the horizon lines of our landscapes.

Fridays were collages. All of us had newspapers to cut. Miss Bell made us read around our pictures, the world's week moving from desk to desk. When a country was named, she showed it on the map that hung like tapestry. She said "Hello" in its language until we heard ourselves right there. When she kept silent, we knew there were places on the earth we should never go.

3

We wrote for reading, making stories
Miss Bell taped to the wall. Our characters
Lived near Pittsburgh in neighborhoods
We could walk to. They watched Ed Sullivan
And *Twenty One*. Their fathers went to work
At seven or three or eleven,
Passing each other in the light or dark.

Covering one blackboard was a map
That showed every street in our town.
On all of them were squares that stood
For houses where our stories happened.
If we were good enough, she said,
We could make others see the rooms.
If we were wonderful, our readers
Could find their way out in the dark.

"Make us believe," Miss Bell encouraged.
"Make us care." And we gave our mothers
Daily sadness, our fathers despair.
When our children feared the future,
She doled out praise. "Make it real," she said,
And we put in bars and cigarettes,
Injuries at work. I added sickness,
A hospital, doctors and nurses who
Couldn't help. "The secret word is *trouble*,"
She said. Every good story starts there.

4

Science was war, Miss Bell said. Soon enough, we'd know
what she meant by that, each of us with an army on her map
of the world. When we learned the accurate lift of levers, she
advanced our flags. When we forgot the water cycle,
Communists moved closer to our homes. Ronald Benson, by
Christmas, had Soviets in New York. Lorraine Ault had Reds
near Pittsburgh, ten miles away. In Poland, the winter hard,
my troops readied to march on Moscow and finish things off
by spring.

January was the battle of electricity, AC/DC and the reason our lightbulbs let us learn in the dark. "Filaments," she whispered. Incandescent. Amperes. Ohms. This was the way into the Soviet Union, Leningrad another one hundred percent away. Prepared to cross the border, I drew the engine of a battery. The room was an atlas surrounded by our art.

5

Miss Bell, during music, said we were blessed
To be born under a fortunate flag,
And she listened to us sing, one by one,
The *National Anthem* we'd memorized
For September because she'd prepared us
A calendar of songs: *America*
For October; *Over There,* November;
And *The Battle Hymn of the Republic*
To celebrate Christmas in our country.

She placed us exactly under the flag.
She showed us the posture to duplicate,
Her back as straight as a poster soldier's.
We listened, not laughing, to Dick Kress sing
Soprano; we clapped for Anne Roth, who cried,
All of us staring at the back windows
To look patriotic and proud, working
Our way through a capella praise for home.

We sang perfectly in our heads, pushing
The verses forward like our Sunday creeds,
The slow and the smart all celebrating

The great chance we had been given by God.
Miss Bell pitch-piped us to song through April,
When she vanished into cancer, leaving
The *Air Force Hymn* for May, a substitute
For whom we sang in unison, keeping
Our pledge to be perfect, voices soaring
Like the planes that protected the cities
In forty-eight states half of us could name
In order, all of our parents saying
This was a lesson we needed to learn,
No matter if we could carry a tune,
And no matter if some of our voices
Swept down from boy to man and back again.

The Impossible

Like Ours

Ninety-two students and three nuns died in a
school fire in Chicago on December 1, 1958.

For days after the fire, we talked about
Our Lady of the Angels school, how boys
And girls like us had died in their classrooms.

Miss Anderson said that school, like ours, was
A chimney, and we needed, each of us,
To pay attention now, lips zipped and sealed.

They had one unreachable fire escape,
Wooden walls and floors like ours, years of wax
Building rectangular plains of candles.

She said the common corridor we used
Would be impossible with smoke, and we
Listened, so quiet, already like ghosts.

Their windows, she told us, were tall, their sills,
Like ours, twenty-five feet from the pavement,
Our fall the same as Catholic children

Whose parents paid to keep them safe from schools
Like ours, where nuns and priests were characters
In jokes that featured discipline or sex.

"Readiness," she said. "Remember." And when
The bell slapped us, a ruler to the wrist,
We lurched up as we did for pledge and prayer.

Outside, rain was freezing, weather so bad
The alarm seemed real. Like ours, their school day
Was almost over. Like ours, their weekend

Was beginning. "Calmly," she said. "Now go."
The sleet slicked the fire escape's iron steps
And our uncovered heads until eighteen

Of us, silently descending, broke loose
From the brick wall, our bodies flung against
A railing that rescued us like firemen.

"Hurry now," she said, "go down," and we did,
Assembling like a choir, everybody
Singing the same chorus that morning, safe

Until we climbed the main stairs to our room
From which, like theirs, no exit existed
But the long, luminous stride into air.

Decorative Food

Using "the new design for happiness,"
My mother cooked meals by Betty Crocker.
She stuffed pie shells and peppers, filled pastry
Sculpted into flowers, made steak from beef
And cereal, a carrot strip for bone.

For holidays, she shaped jellos and cakes
Into flags and ghosts. At Christmas,
Her cookies showed the gentle face of Christ,
Though once, as duty, my mother hosted
A minister who preached the death of God.

He sat, so heavy, against our table,
While her spokes of celery seemed to churn
On their cucumber cogs. As we folded
Our hands, he helped himself to corn and beans.
While my father offered thanks for the care

With which our food was prepared, he buttered
A roll, and then we raised our heads to paint
Our bread with mustard or mayonnaise and
Added roll-ups of meat and cheese, each one
Shaped like the pipes of an organ I heard

While God's obituary ascended
From the stories that pastor presented,
Calling himself a coroner, saying

My father's prayer was delivered to ears
In God's old grave or to nothing at all.

Nobody turned on the overhead light
In our kitchen. The evening leaked inside
Until the minister faded. Voices
Blew out like candles; the thin smiles of talk
Wafted through the screens and vanished like souls.

Houses with No Television

At first, uncommon. Then so quickly rare,
Houses without television became
Whooping cranes or condors, large things passing
From our lives—Frank Derr's, where his parents watched
The perpetual broadcast of absence.
They had packed bookshelves along three full walls,
Magazines arranged so thickly, they looked
Like the office subscriptions of doctors.
Like his mother worked there. Like his father
Sat behind a door keeping appointments
With people who read to keep fear confused.
Across from their green couch was a space where
A television belonged, the carpet
Bright where no one walked. That spot, unused, looked
Like a room built for a child suddenly
Stillborn, the family passing that door,
Seeing furniture doggedly waiting
Until it turned impossible to use,
Someone, then, closing that door so the room
Turned into the idea of a child,
And then, at last, a dark, unheated space,
A draft slipping under the door, something
Noted when a woman paused while passing,
Uncomfortable only if she stopped
And sat with her back against it, the chill
Using the language of the imagined.

English Class Report:
I Married a Monster from Outer Space

He has to marry her. Nothing
Unusual in that, loveless
For the sake of children,
But think of going home
To the horror of something
That can't leave you alone.

How did he get into this skin?
No star-flight boot camp
For invasion had prepared him
For this bad luck, drawing
The short straw of beauty
As his extraterrestrial duty.

Lust, arousal, foreplay—
His mind's being fed by a fool.
Everything in his head is
Thighs and lips, breasts and hips,
But something's not getting through;
She's pliable as fish, smooth

As a nausea of eggs, and
Finally, he's sick of acting.
Outside of town, in the spaceship,
Is the man who wants to drown
Under her, smother her from above—
Telepathy can be reversed.

Let him listen for a while
As he walks upstairs to bed,
His body changing to knobs
And ridges, his face to tubes.
He knows that every planet
Has fables of tested love,

And just then, before he turns
The corner, he hears her
Undressing, and he breathes
One moment from the reason
For exploring, spending all
Of those light years on travel.

The Theory of Dog Shit

Jack McLeod proved the theory of dog shit,
How a burning bag full drew people
We hated to their front porches where
Fathers, especially, stamped out fire
While we watched from the nearest shadows.
Better yet, there were men wearing white shirts
Who cursed into the darkness, calling us
Cocksuckers, faggots, and fucking assholes,
Teaching the great obscenities of rage.
And best, as if his words were sonar,
One man hurtled directly at us.
At eleven o'clock, Friday night,
He was wearing cuff links and a tie,
Deserving shit on his gleaming shoes,
We thought, for sporting that costume so late.
And though both of us wanted to bolt,
We knew his path was an accident,
That if we stayed behind the junipers
We could watch him slow down, stop, and scream
Again, adding "I know you're out there"
To each scatological expletive
While we crouched in the dark and memorized
The reusable language of the stained.

White Gloves

Going out meant church, my mother,
Like a surgeon, slipping on white gloves
At the door. They said she was ready;
They said get in the car, sit in back,
And, *Remember*, keep the window up.

She held a tissue to the handles
And knobs between our house and our pew.
She wore them once and washed them; she owned
A second, identical pair,
Three ridges along the back that matched

The two pairs in boxes she'd wear new
For Easter or Christmas or weddings
That required her extended hands.
White gloves, she said, were like glasses,
What she needed to see past herself.

The president's beautiful wife wore
White gloves like lipstick, her newsreel hands
Bleached by public expectation,
But after Dallas, my mother
Entered her Sundays without them.

She prayed with her fingers touching
Until only old women were white
To the wrists, and she died, three pairs
In the drawer of her last things, two pairs
Waiting in boxes like the souls

Of the unborn, so patient, so long,
Like lamps left on after the day
Enters through windows, light unnoticed
Until evening when we're surprised
And say to ourselves, *Remember.*

Skill

Just often enough somebody comes back
From certain death, enough to make us think
We're the ones who will go on, like my friend
Thrown clear of the T-Bird that exploded
On impact, the neighbor's boy who survived
Ten minutes under cold water, even
Myself skidding into a four-wheel drift
Across a low median and both lanes
Of oncoming, rush-hour freeway traffic.
Unscathed. Upright. Not miraculous. Not
A free fall ten thousand feet to a swamp.
Not, the week I rejoined traffic and kept
Close escape to myself, the young pilot
Bringing in the plane with the blown hatch door,
Ferrying a full manifest of ghosts
Back to the everyday task of living.

Safely on earth, the one in a thousand,
He spoke about trying to keep that plane
Alive, throttling up, working the small chance
Of improvisation while it banked left
And dived, drawn sideways and down by its wound.
"If I land this thing," he said to laughter,
Was the first phrase of a hurried promise
That ended with "all the rest of my life."
And then he started the full-time labor
Of silence about how, after those first

Minutes of surviving, he knew he would
Never again be so skillful, that it
Saddened him until he seemed an athlete
Just retired, his gratitude so awkward
And false he knew this was the first day of
The long sentence of dissatisfaction.

Glitter Stars

With Old Testament prophets on the left hand,
With New Testament disciples to the right,
The design sung by the angels visiting
Washington, while James Hampton constructed
A throne room for the second coming of Christ.
With aluminum foil, with kraft paper,
With the gold glitter of packaging for wine
And cigarettes and chocolate candy,
With all of the thirteen years the public schools
And my parents worked to make me worth saving,
He formed cardboard and plywood to prepare
A ceremonial setting for the Lord.
With insulation board. With desk blotters.
With failed light bulbs and outcast jelly jars.
With the inventory of the dumpster,
The fervor of finding each object holy.
With dedication. With faith. With cold and heat.
With sickness and fatigue. With the minutes
Someone else formed foil into a planet
Of scraps. With the hours someone else wound thread
Into an enormous ball. With the late nights
I worked with my father in his bakery
To form bread and cake from a million fragments.

With matched icons to attract a gold bolt
Of Christ's descent while I dreamed the glitter stars
Of success, the bright As of achievement,

And couldn't build anything with my hands
Except stacks of assigned books while I wanted
To be the film aliens who moved objects
With their minds and stacked our army's weapons
As a definitive, first line of defense.
With mild oaths while I parried the fists
Of classmates who walked the halls with failure's fever,
Laying their hot hands flush to my honors face.
With original prayers and hymns sung
To the great God of imminent return
While all the lyrics I loved turned tumescent
With lust, each melody smoking cigarettes,
Drinking beer, and loving the pinball of sequins
And lamé; while all the verses wanted
Breasts and thighs, and I brought a thousand pop
Records into my room where returning Jesus
Would find me memorizing the simple chords
For desire and angst, repeating them like litanies
I heard twice a week from my family's pew.

With anthems and cantatas. With chanted creeds.
With the beatitudes of blessed are
The builder's hands, blessed is the throne room
Formed with the refuse of temporary rule,
Blessed are those who believe in the sweet voice
Which whispers *Yes*. Now, James Hampton was telling
Himself in 1964, Christ will strip
This warehouse roof, open this dazzling throne room.
Now, the gathering of souls will shield their eyes

And blink through the final state of the union
Address in heaven's bi-figured conference room.
Now, I echoed, packing for college, taking
What I wanted from my gilded room, leaving
With clothes, with trophies, with every record
I warbled with the Robins, with the Blue Jays,
With the Orioles, Ravens, and Cardinals
Through the bi-figured world of A and F,
Crew cut and duck tail, pen and fists; each record
Replayed by lifting the needle, placing it
Where pop and crackle signaled the second
Before harmonies began, never knowing
Of Hampton unlocking the door to glory,
Depicting its symmetry under the pull string
Of the bare light bulb above the golden throne.

Woom! Ball

We circled at three a.m., just before the two-mile run, fifteen pledges who slammed a football broadside into our neighbors' guts. Woom! we said, and cupped our hands like running backs to keep ourselves from harm. Woom! There were pledges who moaned. Pledges who doubled up and wished this half hour gone. Woom! There were brothers who joined, standing beside the pledges who never showed fear or pain.

Woom! We fired back, driving that ball into the stomach of seniors just returned drunk from bars. Woom! Until Jim Ulsh took that ball point first and came apart inside. Woom! Until Dave Mazur cracked a rib because that ball thunked wide. We were five days into the week of no sleep. We were nearly finished with Woom! ball, one more night, and I was left standing beside Cecil Clifford, who screamed Woom! like a sound could take the air out of me, neither of us knowing he would die in a war that was as small, that night, as our skirmish. Woom! I shouted, and nobody stepped between us until that circle broke for the road where we ran into the town that was sleeping, watching for lights in windows at quarter to four, guessing whether whoever moved there was coming home from trouble or waking into a day that, starting this early, meant pain.

Girdles

Coming of age at the end of the girdle era,
I'd touched nothing, on the way to pleasure, but cotton
Or silk until one night, under a girl's dress, I was
Fumbling through a set of unfamiliar keys, cold wind
Numbing my ungloved hands until I rubbed against her
In anxiety and lust, shooting in a shudder
Of shame upon that beige, impenetrable armor.

I began to drive while she used four Kleenex she dropped
Onto the floor of my father's Chevrolet, leaving
Them for me to remember or forget. I went back,
The next morning, to my second semester, and she,
By June, was engaged, so sudden and definitive
That news from my mother, I uttered an *Oh* of loss.

For sure, she was in the family way, my mother said,
But all along she'd sung in the choir as if alto
Were the voice of abstinence, her harmonies washing
Past my mother's shoulder until she began to show,
And what did I think of that—hadn't she been a friend?

My answer? I turned away until the night after
My mother died, opening her drawers like a husband,
Guessing at, when I came to one girdle, the last time
She'd worn it, whether before or after that choir girl
Had packed hers away with training bras and petticoats.

Twenty-seven years had passed since I'd touched one,
            and when
I laid my hand on its strange surface, the bedroom filled
So deep with violation I felt like a rapist,
Like I'd torn that girl's pale, unfathomable girdle
From her hips, so much in need of being inside her
I didn't care if she sang me her pleasure or screamed.

Because It Was Always Summer

Because it was always summer when work
Was measured for me by the union's scale,
Because I believed school would end my shift
For good, I punched out and stood among men
Years older and waited for those strangers
To decide the afternoon's direction.

Since seven o'clock, in sterilizing,
I'd worked with them at Heinz, a fog of steam
Forming and fading through measured cycles
That protected whoever ate the soup
Condensed inside a hundred thousand cans.

Always the same men talked, and the same men
Nodded or shook their heads, swallowing shots
And downing chasers from glasses before
They lifted their eyes to the bartender
Who knew their signals like an auctioneer.
There wasn't a TV or a juke box,
Just men who wanted to talk or listen
Or be left alone, knowing whoever
Was on screen or a record could care less
About men who worked with their hands and backs.

The dog that roamed that after-work tavern
Knew enough not to beg for bits of bun
Or hamburger, that even a dog should
Act as if it needed nothing, because

It would come, eventually, like crumbs.
I waited weeks to say something about
Myself, what college was, a way to work
Without wearing a boss like a stiff suit.

The dog lifted its head to my new voice;
A man two stools from mine said, "Fuck college."
July kept passing outside. A bus hissed
And collected three men who left a space
Near the door. The rest of us were driving,
Deciding two things for ourselves, the when
Of leaving and what we would listen to
After we pointed our cars toward some part
Of Pittsburgh, selecting which stranger's voice
Might comfort us while we worked our way home.

The Impossible

College down to its final semester,
It was, I vowed, my last winter of walking
In terrible weather. The mornings I slogged
Through snow, I thought I could see myself
In the near future of beating the draft,
Shuffling from the physical with the joy
Of a small, but unacceptable flaw.
In Florida, where I planned to be,
Three astronauts were killed on the ground,
Inhaling the toxic smoke of a flash fire,
Their deaths grafting them to my classmate
Crushed by a jeep in basic training,
All the danger of the war months away.
That weekend, stopped by sirens, I learned
A girl who had said goodbye to me
Had died in the car she'd chosen thirteen miles
Before, that whatever else she'd meant
To say had been hurled through a windshield.

Like she could have been, I was riding
With Cecil Clifford, who was going
To explode in the air over Vietnam,
But right then, just after two a.m., we shared
The expletives that follow sudden death.
Added the sentences full of *if,*
The paragraphs stuffed with stories meant as
Consolations for what seemed impossible—
To die so fast surrounded by rescue.
On the news, January shutting down,

Were tributes to Grissom, Chaffee, and White.
February filled with fault speculations
About frayed wires, oxygen level, the hatch
Too difficult to reach, and I told myself
I wanted to hear what that sophomore,
The driver, had to say about speed and ice
And drinking because even I had known
Enough to rely on the judgment
Of Cecil Clifford the way I relied
On somebody every night when what
I wanted was more than two miles from school,
Riding in five cars a week, half of them
Driven by soldiers-to-be, without
Saying a word about the test flights
We were taking to decide what was worth it,
What was not, turning up the radio
So impossibly loud a siren
Couldn't slow any of us who believed
We were learning quickly enough to live.

The Shooting

Kent, Ohio

I sat, this morning, on the grass
Where thirty-five years ago
I survived the guardsmen's volley.
I sprawled beside a parking lot
So long I wondered why no one
Asked me why. I could see the small,
Stone memorial to four dead
Students, the pagoda unchanged
On the hill's horizon. What was
I expecting while I became
My father crossing the landfilled
Lot of his long-closed bakery
And naming the gunman who thought
Sixty dollars would change his life?
Who was watching while I became
My grandfather walking the mile
Of his lost mill where strikebreakers
Succeeded once, then failed? Something
Stood on these fields and then was gone—
Ovens, cranes, armed men in gas masks,
The work we did from steel to bread
To books. I told myself I'd sit
Until somebody asked me why,
And morning slid past noon, women
And men moving to cars, pulling
Away, unwilling to question.

Mother's Day, 1970

"They should have shot you, too," my uncle said,
After I chose between the protesters
And the blunt authority of the Guard.
Sick of my mutton chops and thick mustache,
He hated how I thought I knew the world
Better than he did without picking up
A gun or grenade or the requisite
Gumption to wear a uniform with pride.
That Sunday I was back home from Kent State
Where classes had been canceled on account
Of jerks and whiners like me. My father,
The one brother of four who hadn't aimed
And fired at Nazis, sat silently through
That long oral exam for loyalty,
My uncle repeating "Look at yourself,"
Like a self-taught family therapist,
Waiting while I drifted to France where men
Who had followed him were guessing their odds
Against the higher ground of the Fascists,
Each of those men staring at my uncle
For the terrible, opened lips of "Go."

All Through May, 1970

I hitchhiked, believing in the kingdom
Of rootlessness. I was naming myself
By choices, whether I wanted to be
Wounded or dead or the distance runner
Of regret. I carried a small, silly
Suitcase for personal items, saying
Nothing to bored or curious drivers
About my history of presidents
By name: Kennedy, the office-buyer;
Johnson, the quitter; Nixon, the liar,
Who had called my classmates "bums" and killed them
Three hundred yards from my classroom at Kent.
I was waging the old revolution
Of flight, using the pity of strangers
And all of the name-calling that followed
Whiskey chased by beer. By the beginning
Of June, I rode home to re-up at Heinz,
Earning enough to begin my last term
Of accepting the lectures of others.

The Summer After

I wore the company's washed boots.
I jammed my hair inside my hat
And pinned it like the old women
Who were first to arrive at church.

I worked fourteen cooling kettles
And carried long-stemmed spatulas
To scrape a shift's mixed cubes of meat
And vegetables, shake loose the salt.

I worked spaghetti with hot dogs,
Friday, four thirty, the day shift
Backed up at three lights I could see
From the seventh story for soup.

That summer, there were new bosses
Back from the war that wanted me
As soon as I filled my transcript.
They sent me into boxcars where

The split bags of dried beans and flour
Roiled white dust around my face.
My second week, I had to kneel
In watery blood to unclog

A set of drains. For half a shift,
Pairs of men had hoisted frozen
Beef slabs, one hundred pounds per lift,
And they were long sick of wading

Ankle-deep. One veteran boss
Repeated, "Clear the fucking things,"
Adding "Use your fingers" for flesh
Half fat that thawed into the shape

And size of a hundred drain holes.
I felt for meat and pulled it free.
On the loading docks, the lifters
Faced the street to smoke. The warehouse

Rose so close; the sun's shift, in June,
Shone only from ten until two.

Late August

At intermission, when smiling families
Flickered into the trees from the edges
Of the huge screen at Ranalli's Drive-In,
I rinsed my mouth with whisky and hooted
At the teenagers who sipped their soft drinks
While happy-face snack foods skipped to the stars.
I needed to piss and pay for something
Salty for Faye, who wanted to see what
Happened to Steve McQueen. In the men's room,
The cinderblocks repeated *Suck my dick;*
The six light bulbs were yellow, one of them
Overhead when I leaned down to vomit
In the sink, my face jammed beneath the faucet
Until some high school boy in tie-dyed shorts
Looked so long I ripped my knees, right, then left,
Into the middle of his colored crotch.
The boy said "Unhhh" and sat. Outside, Faye stood
In line for popcorn and fries we carried
Past a Plymouth where James Brown was groaning
"Hot Pants" as if he were fondling her hips.
Our speaker was face down in the gravel.
On the screen four hamburgers were dancing
Among cheerful cups of Coke. I lifted
The damp cord, and the tinny trumpets that
Moved their cartoon feet heaved up between us.

After School Reopened

The students who had died
Brought me old tests and papers;
They'd cleaned out their rooms
And wanted me to file their work
Graded A through F in stacks.
There's no turning down the dead—
Some mornings, a box of scrawls
Sat outside the door. Finally,
The names were torn off, paragraphs
Missing, leaving me to decide
How they began and ended,
Who wrote each one and why.
On my Kent, Ohio, street
Lived a woman whose garage
Was full of found shoes. "Local,"
She told me, "all of them, so it's
Just a matter of time to match."
She showed me a two-tiered shelf.
"So far," she said, "six pairs,
This last one taking a year
To mate," something to tell
The months-dead plagiarist
Who dared our teacher to prove it:
"Where," he said, "in all the world,
Are you going to look?"

Winter: The Barter System

After he hit me, the drunk in the truck
Offered fifty-five dollars and a gun.
He said, "Ok now, no need for police."
Though there was a left headlight to replace,
A fender to wrestle back from the tire.
On the highway, at two a.m., zero
Settling upon us like snow, I didn't
Negotiate because I thought I was
Getting an investment back with interest.
A month before I'd paid fifty dollars,
Total, for that car with steering problems,
And the truth is, I'd been out drinking, too,
My sober-by-comparison nothing
The police would credit. For five months more
I drove that fifty-dollar car until
It leaked oil so badly I drove it
Into a thick-trunked tree to make it quit.
That gun? I kept it in a dresser drawer
Like something loaded with caps. Before then,
I had fired one twenty-two in my life,
Hitting dirt three times before surprising
The fluttering edge of a pillow case
Tacked to a tree stump on my uncle's farm.
Finally, I needed ammunition
To get my barter's worth, and I carried
That pistol to a store to size bullets
To barrel, the clerk turning it over
And over in his hands as if he were

Memorizing the serial number
To match a police report on his desk.
"You shoot this here thing and you fixing to
Fuck yourself up," that salesman said at last,
Showing me the crack, how it ran so straight
I'd seen it as design. "Billy the Kid,"
He said, "be cool," and I inventoried
That specialty store like a thief, counting
Three customers, figuring which of them
Would haul my lame story home, including
How flushed I turned, how quickly I beat it
To that car I'd wreck for good in two weeks.
For miles, I steadied at the speed-limit,
Checked my mirrors and turned the radio
To murmur, driving ten minutes to where
I flung that pistol off a bridge, timing
The spaced headlights of witnesses until
I was free, in the dark, to let it go.

The Anniversaries

Year after year, in May, I read
The wire service for Kent State news.
The veterans spoke sadly, stunned
In the empty spring. They retold
For students required to attend,
Assistants taking roll beside
The single security man
Who clocked the permitted time.
My short, annual story
Of not returning ended
In car doors closing. Seven
Of those years it was raining
When I walked outside, counting down
The minutes in Pennsylvania
And then New York, saying "Now,"
Listening to wind and traffic.

The Casual Slurs

Early in an evening of remembering death,
I tell my friend that after the Kent State shooting,
After students like me went home and waited out
Our anger, the police came armed to Jackson State
Like a recreation of the Ohio Guard.
They herded those students, I tell him. They backed them
Against the front wall of a dorm and suffered stones
And bricks until they opened fire as if they'd loved
The headlines from the week before, emulating
The Midwest's faux-army, sustaining their gunfire
Thirty seconds with an armory of weapons.

Almost five hundred times, I say, they hit that dorm.
Two dead, twelve wounded, all of them "nigger students"
According to the cop who called in the shooting.
That speaker's nickname was "Goon," something history
Can't make up, his casual slurs, on tape, leaching
Into the voiceless future to poison language,
The violent separations that mark our speech
Though we've forgotten their indecipherable
Beginnings, ones like birth and the early years, what
We hear about from the mouths of those who love us.

History Bites

One night, in his room, complaining, my son
Sat to steal his report from the *World Book*,
List the Kent State dates and dead like fractions
To be reduced. "History Bites," it said
On his paper, "choose one, taste, and swallow,"
And I surprised him with slides, his father
The student who'd sampled his fresh mouthful
Of wartime after class. Monday, May 4,
Returned on his wall, and he worked the crowd
For someone familiar from the dark age
Of flared pants, long hair, and armies. Though I
Was faculty by now, standing in front
Of students with the rifle of language,
I wanted to show myself on his wall
Like some shadow animal of the hands—
Rabbit of the fingers, the knuckled dog,
Decorative pain of the headstone past.
"Look, there I am then," I said, history
Whirring in that projector's fan. My son
Said, "What were you doing?" and I managed
"Watching," followed silence with "I don't know"
As if he were asking why I'd never
Left college or written a single word
On history as it happened, a roar
Of oaths and gestures raising those rifles.
And what I told my son was "Write this down":

We thought they were blanks; we stood ignorant
As some lost tribe staring at sticks that smoked.
Which is the way these histories happen,
Somebody saying "Never," "Of course not,"
Or its thousand variants. The crowd scene
That follows, the jostling forward of trust.

The Ghosts in the Shelter

Something like the Attic

I'm up, as always, before the first light
With the dark birds I can't identify,
The ones that crowd our maple like a mob.
5:05, July, like the time in red
On the clock radio when I awoke
For the 6:15 to 3 shift at Heinz
Where I worked for two summers, shoveling,
For weeks, dried beans that spilled from broken bags
In boxcars, cleaning up while Funovitz,
The forklift man, parked on the dock to smoke
Because his seniority had earned it.
I looked for rats as I filled the short tubs,
Inhaling the white dust inside something
Like the attic where my father would sleep
To ready himself for night shift, his sheets
Stained so often by sweat they turned yellow,
My mother said, "As if he pissed the bed."
Weekends, he slept with her on the pull-out
In the middle room of three we rented,
Lying on the white sheets my mother ironed,
On the pillowcases with pink roses
I sometimes saw before my mother slid
Shut the heavy, Saturday evening door,
The thick panel that stayed open all week,
My mother always awake, no matter
How early I rose, even in the dark,
The attic closed against the stink of sleep
And sweat, my mother saying "Listen now,"

Turning me toward the brown birds that nested
On our windowsills, the ones we could hear
Until the traffic to Pittsburgh thickened,
Backed up from the stoplight three blocks away,
Starting to build a neighborhood of horns
And engines in the blue air of morning.

Love Poem for the Dying

On this dangerous street, eight houses long,
Half the husbands' hearts have had surgery.
On Saturdays, through summer, one neighbor
Strides shirtless behind his mower, and I
Can read, from my congruent route, the scars
From that autobiography of blood.

Across the road, his car covered with snow,
The music teacher's home from Buffalo,
From the cancer clinic where lasers cleaned
His liver and kidneys, his maples wrapped
In so many jaundiced ribbons he might
Have sons at war. And I think of how he

Watches me walk my skittish Spitz, retrieve
My mail the way I've done the thirty days
He's been gone. How I lived near Buffalo
For five winters of whiteouts, wind-blown snow
Guaranteed each year. How all of our cells
Meet their schedules, turning off like timed bulbs

In the living rooms of vacationers.
How the art of aging has been tested
By the careful critique of fibroblasts:
Divide and double, divide and double,
Those cells keeping a sculler's pace because
Deceleration means decay, because

The end of the steady doublings is death.
Here they stop at fifty; here fifteen; here
Ninety: Human. Mouse. Tortoise. Which give us
The variables for genetic math,
All of those cells reading the DNA
Novel from conception to senescence

As if our hearts and kidneys and livers
Weren't strangled by the accidental cords.
As if the natural death for language
Were untallied, words like these dividing
And doubling in rhythmic, exacting ways—
Genes as similes, DNA symbols

For heaving ourselves forward through futures
With the oblique force of learning, knowing
Someone, now, is working to fool our genes,
Produce a kind of daylight savings time
For our body-clocks, so, scarcely aging,
We will smother the incredulous earth.

The Ghosts in the Shelter

The realtor says, "Your very own cold war museum,"
Because under the back yard, accessible still,
Is the room a family built into the earth.

She shows us a cover that could lead to a well;
She reveals there's a key on a hook by the door
Out of which that family expected to flee.

For however long it took, those planners-ahead
Were willing to hide from the air. Five hundred cans
Of food might last a year. So could water by the gallon,

Three decks of cards, the library of favorite books
And board games. Now those parents and their children are
The things returning to earth; the missile crisis

Is a paragraph in a textbook, a movie,
Or nothing at all, my wife and the young realtor
Talking on the back porch while I carry that key

To the horizontal door, becoming sixteen
Underground, my sister fifteen and outliving
Every girl I desire until she becomes them.

And what of her longing? And what of our parents
At forty-three listening to static so long
There's no need to reascend in the buttoned clothes

Of modesty? To become that family, the world
Had to erupt, the inevitable that has
Not happened, not yet, leaving their hands untested.

The room speaks the familiar language of collapse,
The alliteration of must and mold, mildew
And my thinking, when I close that door, "Just to see,"

Beginning at once to doubt even my breathing,
Deciphering nothing for so long I vanish,
Understanding the first necessity is light.

Such Places

When my mother talked about sickness,
She named the foreign diseases
We would not get: Elephantiasis,
Yellow fever, cholera, yaws.
"Such places," she said, and I have never
Traveled to one of those countries where
The world's worst maladies begin.
I've never entered a jungle where
Men bleed from their pores or women swell
Into monstrous clouds. I've stayed at home
And seen no one die but four students
At Kent State by means other than disease.
When I talk about sickness, I mention
My mother and her sister and the rest
Of my family who slipped silently
To death. I mean their shattered hearts
Or the sudden lightning of massive stroke.
My wife adds hidden tumors, how we've named
The three for which we've been tested—
CAT scans, bone scans, both our wired bodies
Walking the treadmill for the EKG
After we listened so passively
To our pleasant doctors, we suffered
The pursed lips of the terminal.

Still negative, we think of the worst
Diseases we've really had, pneumonia
And rheumatic fever, guessing
Our odds in the outback, but when

Our son finally speaks, he describes
AIDS at the health club where he works,
The lesioned intruder he asked to leave.
Because he was naked, our son says,
Because he was drunk and broke the rules,
Almost as skinny as the anorexic
Who did sit ups in the sauna,
Weighing herself six times per hour.
So many ways our bodies can be
Entered, so many exotic names:
Ebola, Lassa, Marburg, Machupo—
They sound like a roster of devils. No,
They sound like the angels of anxiety
Who manifest themselves to the healthy.

The 1918 House

My father, whose limp is a stutter,
Says he was born in the epidemic,
The early days, when people survived
As expected because it was just flu.

In May, he tells me, the cases were
Three-day fevers. By June, he says, the flu
Had moved to where it always summers,
Far from the warm weather of families.

My father, who shuffles like those who
Are stared at by children, accepts my hand
For surfaces other than sidewalks
To examine every place where he's lived.

In September, he tells me, symptoms
Meant death—the coughing of blood, the blue face,
The darkening of feet that said *soon*
In the common language for conclusion.

The lungs, he says, went soggy with blood;
The people drowned for days. The newly born,
He murmurs, were passed over like sons
Of Jews, God's mercy on their infant breath.

My father, who refuses a cane,
Touches a wall he built in a yard owned
By strangers, pausing on his way to
The beginning, the house where, in the year

Of the Spanish flu, he was first-born
And no one died, where his parents survived
To see themselves chosen, praising God
And good fortune and their lifetimes of work.

On both sides, he says, are the houses
Of victims, sons who enlisted for war,
And he pauses, the porch so different
I have to read the number to prove it.

How winter blessed us, he says, ending
That horror, driving us inside to love.
He asks me to knock on the white door;
He says these people will invite us in.

This

"Keep this," my father writes. "It's the last card
you'll get from me." I have a collection—
from Christmas, Easter, Thanksgiving, birthdays.

He empties his house, gives furniture to
strangers. "Take this," he says, offering me
frozen food that must keep two hundred miles.

He stuffs suits in my car, fills the front seat
with shoes. "Wear this," he says, meaning old ties
and a sweatshirt abandoned years ago.

He's proud to show two bare rooms, a garage
without a tool. The newspaper passes
in a schoolboy's sack; magazines expire.

Behind us, the sun slides to memory.
The shadows we cast slip into our shoes.
"I'm ready for this," he says, but doesn't

follow me to the driveway. As if he
means me to see how everything will look
without him, he's vanished when I reach my car.

The Empowerment of Trust

When one student wrote about the empowerment
Of trust, how twenty other young women believed
They were stronger because a professor taught them
To confess and led the class in unison screams,
I told her I'd taken a trust walk for credit,
That some woman who taught history had led me,
Blindfolded, to the smooth edge of a high school stage
And turned me in a circle. "Take three steps forward,"
She'd said, "because, trust me, your back is to the fall."
Staring at darkness, I'd told her about the man
Who'd suddenly about-faced and goose-stepped off a cliff,
Certain he'd outsmarted his calculating guide.
Once, twice, I blew out the bad air of doubt, fluttered
In place until she said, "It's quite all right," then paused,
Silently breathing, and drew the cloth from my eyes.

My student smiled and waited, but I was lying
Like a teacher. What did I want from role-playing?
To tell her I watched seven friends gangbang a girl
Her age who picked the wrong afternoon to be drunk?
That there are enough tales of lost trust to complete
The canon of despair? My job, some mornings, is
To scratch words like *anomaly* and *distancing*
On a blackboard so a row of hands can record
The vocabulary they pay for. I wanted
To say I didn't take a turn, but the truth is
That girl puked from chugging beer before my number,
And I saw myself so sick and small I could say
The horrible, hushed *no* of leaving. That I lived,

Afterward, with those friends for years. That most of them
Joked about the bad lay of the vomiting bitch,
And the worst rebuke was silence. That thirty years
Later, reuniting, I never once brought up
That rape and the absence of remorse. Already,
Two of those seven friends had died. I had to ask
The names of two others who'd aged so terribly
They looked like patients. I repeated that story,
And I had a photograph to prove it, showing
My student a set of strangers who had returned
To a crime scene because it stood for something else.

Heavy Fog, December

Near December's end, the news carries
Jesus sightings, messiahs fathered
By wood grain, Christs created by light
And shadow. In this cemetery,
A display of Christmas lights gone up,
Cars come for Santas and elves, snowmen,
Angels, their forms unfocused by fog
From warmth improbable as the priest
In South Africa who is suing
His surgeon for erasing his soul
During three hours of heart surgery.

Belief, he says, is a cave drawing
That disappears when exposed to light,
And I think of Abbé Henri Breuil,
Who copied cave drawings sixty years
And studied them, predicting the growth
Of art would be chronological,
From the simple and crude to complex,
How man progresses, he thought, to God.

And though some could be traced on paper
Laid over them on cave walls, he found
Pigments so miraculously moist
They came off on contact, forcing him
To his back, under the cave ceilings,
Where he sketched those fragile renderings
Because photography, too, wouldn't
Work in the weak light he could carry.

Soon after dusk, the cars nose forward
From a gate where they pay ten dollars,
But now, at noon, I drive through for free.
Who spent November draping these frames
With colored lights? Maude Martz, whose stone says
She died last week, did she dream herself
Rising to see, taking the six steps
From her grave to the snowman couple?

My friend, riding with me, says his wife,
Dead for years, explains how loneliness
Rubs off as easily as cave art,
And I tell him science has dated
Those drawings differently than Breuil,
The oldest most sophisticated,
As if we required less from art
After we created eternity.

The Pause in the Plummet for Prayer

They'd plunged thousands of feet, crash-certain, and now,
Miles above the Pacific, a passenger
Walked the aisle like a stewardess. "Let us pray,"
She said, and believers, those passengers did,
Filling the inexplicable nine minutes
Of frail stability with supplication.
That plane scribbled like a toddler on the sky
While every one of them felt saved, we're told, Flight
Two Sixty-One's miracle joining the best
Stories that begin *Did you know. . .?* passed forward
By the bucket brigade of word-of-mouth, and
Emptied, sent back by the living, retraced from
Here to there to witnesses who cannot speak.

No matter the disaster stories we hear
And repeat, a marvel of wishes spreads from
Our words—healings, sightings, the necessary
Resurrections growing like the hybrid tree
We planted, in seven years the tallest thing
On our street; in seven more so enormous
We took it down, and yet it drives a thousand
Descendants from roots spread the length of our yard.
Our neighbors walk out to a field of saplings
Sprung up like gifts from the magi of desire.
This morning, standing among them, we marvel
At the force of rebirth, how, if everything
Returned, we would stand in the darkness of awe.

Elegy:
The Properties of Blood

Elegy: The Properties of Blood

1963

First among the maxims of medicine
Was always "What you don't know won't hurt you,"
My father speaking, relying on faith,
Though he slumped back, shaking, when the doctor
Probed and cleaned the deep punctures in my knee.

As if anything unnamed was harmless,
He hadn't visited a physician
In twenty years, and then, as he lay down,
His voice sounded like a coward's asking
For one less public backhand in the face.

The doctor murmured a brief lullaby
Of assurance. My leg was nothing but
A day off from practice, nothing that stopped
Me from learning the way blood flattens us,
Rushing from the head like air from spiked tires.

And then, suddenly, I was my father
Surrendering to a weakness, shadowed
By somebody repeating "Ok, now,"
The overhead light turning so clouded
It seemed impossible to remember.

1966

I thought I was heroic, needle in my arm,
Talking to keep myself from imagining death.
My friend's mother needed blood, and I'd tested well
For the first time that spring semester when I risked
Myself drunk-driving half the nights of every week.

Through the mail, in less than a month, the registrar
Would send grades much worse than the B+ of my blood.
The truth is I'd missed my ride home with her because
I'd left early to party, and now I believed

My getting into the car would have delayed her,
That surely stuffing my cheap suitcase in the trunk
Would have added several seconds to her trip,
Enough time to miss the run-through-the-stop-sign car.

Thinking like that is useless, my friend insisted,
And I agreed, foreseeing myself in her seat
Like somebody so selfish I wanted to draw
Volunteers to a hospital to match my blood.

1976

"Make a fist," says the woman who straps my arm,
"Think of what you love," smiling like a waitress,
And yet, as always, I go pale and clammy,
The love of my own body insufficient.

I yammer like an auctioneer for fainting
Until that lab flares and bursts and disappears.

"Here you are again," she says, "back in the world,"
So unsurprised by leaving and coming back,
I know at once that what I've done in darkness
Is routine, every secret confessed by blood.

1986

My cousin says she stores her blood for safety,
Carries it like gum. Accidents, surgeries,
Especially travel in foreign countries.

An investment, she says, a portfolio
Of blood, and I think of precautions for loss,
The pint numbers for security to cross

A border with temporary peace of mind.
"Transfusion insurance," she tells me, one kind
She can purchase, betrayed by blood, her two sons

Stunted by the gene-pool curse of Fragile X.
Stuck for something to say, I read from my text
Of failures, how I faint when my blood comes next,

How my father has passed down a stupid dread.
And she remembers the morning when I bled
From a fall at her house, how she pretended

She was my battlefield nurse. Three years older,
She bandaged my wounds. "So brave when you were four,"
She murmurs now, mistaking trust for valor.

1999

My father has survived the surgeries
That stop the heart, his blood pumped by machine.

Today he repeats his pulse and pressure,
Says *clamps* and *shunts* and *stitches*, makes me press
My fingers on the entrance to repair.

"You never know," he tells me, past eighty.
Without shame, he puts hand to wrist and counts
To seventy to measure a minute.

In the small living room of the unsaid,
Love forms itself into a final shape
Indelible as what we do not say.

2003

Each April, the university blood drive
In the gym. The chairs and the cots. Bags and tubes.
Pulp-free orange juice. Pizza by the square slice.
A host of women who hover like mothers.

Each April, my friend who solicits our blood.
The stupid smile I use like a student late
With assignments. Without hearing his question,
I start my stories of public collapse.

Then he doesn't ask me. Twenty-one years pass
Like canned cautions against bad habits, the ones
That encourage the need for donated blood.
The recipient era hovers like hawks.

Then this year he drives into fatality's
Wrong moment. Weather not a factor. Nor speed.
Nor alcohol nor mechanical failure.
Suddenly, the irrelevancy of blood.

Then no. Then April again and the drawing
Of blood. Then my lying down for the needle
As if a spirit could rise from willing veins.
The sun through the skylight hovers like a prayer.

Miracles

Miracles

1

My father grieves like fish,
Turning away, silent.

He sits among absence,
Remembers like the dead.

Each evening he expects
Sleep to be a passage
Into understanding.

He wakes to his limits.
The cane of prophecy
Grips his astonished hand.

2

God's sadness. All these years,
And no one worthy, not
Yet, of revelation.

Each conversation starts
With loaves and fish, water, wine.

Resurrection reveals
The small wish for more years.

Even ascension churns
The old, limited lust
For family, for love.

3

My mother drew faith from
The tiny miracles
Of self-taught, home repair.

Radios and toasters.
Faucets and toilets. Clocks.

The body can be fixed,
She says, two decades dead.
So much of us is air,

So much is water, we are
Elements, everywhere.